W9-BFM-666

21st Century Skills INNOVATION LIBRARY

FORTNITE:
Scavenging

CHERRY LAKE PUBLISHING • ANN ARBOR, MICHIGAN

by Josh Gregory

CHERRY
LAKE
Publishing

Published in the United States of America by Cherry Lake Publishing
Ann Arbor, Michigan
www.cherrylakepublishing.com

Reading Adviser: Marla Conn MS, Ed., Literacy specialist, Read-Ability, Inc.

Library of Congress Cataloging-in-Publication Data
Names: Gregory, Josh, author.
Title: Fortnite. Scavenging / by Josh Gregory.
Other titles: Scavenging
Description: Ann Arbor, Michigan : Cherry Lake Publishing, 2019. | Series:
   Unofficial guides | Series: 21st century skills innovation library |
   Includes bibliographical references and index. | Audience: Grade 4 to 6.
Identifiers: LCCN 2019003334 | ISBN 9781534148116 (lib. bdg.) |
   ISBN 9781534150973 (pbk.) | ISBN 9781534149540 (pdf) |
   ISBN 9781534152403 (ebook)
Subjects: LCSH: Fortnite (Video game)—Juvenile literature.
Classification: LCC GV1469.35.F67 G746 2019 | DDC 794.8—dc23
LC record available at https://lccn.loc.gov/2019003334

Cherry Lake Publishing would like to acknowledge the work of the Partnership for
21st Century Learning. Please visit www.p21.org for more information.

Printed in the United States of America
Corporate Graphics

Contents

Chapter 1

Items Everywhere

H ave you played *Fortnite* yet? This fun, fast-paced online game has taken the entire world by storm. Its combination of action-packed shooting and creative building make it unlike any

The ability to build your own forts, towers, and other structures sets *Fortnite* apart from any other online battle game.

Every new match of *Fortnite* offers nearly unlimited possibilities.

other video game. Players can spend hours upon hours competing to win matches and unlock new **skins** and **emotes**. More than 200 million people have downloaded it so far, and new players are joining the battle every day.

One of the things that makes *Fortnite* so fun is that no two matches are the same. You never know what's going to happen after you parachute down from the Battle Bus. Your character's appearance changes in every match, and you can drop into a different part of the map every time you play. There are 99 other players in every match, and you can't predict what they will do. You might drop into the middle of a hectic battle. Or you might get a chance to take your time and explore before you run into other players.

Most importantly, you can't predict what kinds of items you will find as you play. Weapons, potions, building materials, and other useful gear are scattered randomly throughout *Fortnite*'s island map. You might

You never know where you'll discover the perfect weapons or other useful items.

find a treasure chest containing a powerful gun in an old shed. Or a few bundles of wood might be lying on the floor in the basement of a suburban house. A llama-shaped piñata atop a wooded hill might contain healing items or grenades.

Finding and collecting these items is a key part of playing *Fortnite*. You will start every match with nothing but a pickaxe. Your first goal will always be to **scavenge** for the tools you need to win. You'll need weapons to defeat other players. You'll also need potions and healing items to keep your character strong after an attack. A variety of building supplies will come in handy so you can construct towers, walls, and other defenses. There are many other things to find as well, from balloons that let you float into the sky to traps that you can set for other players to fall into.

There is no way to memorize which items will show up in which locations on the island. In one match, you might find a powerful sniper rifle in an abandoned gas station. But if you visit the same gas station in your next match, you might find a grenade. Or some bandages. Or nothing at all! This might seem frustrating at first, especially if you find a really great item in one match but never get to use it. But as you play more, you'll see that scavenging is a big part of the fun in *Fortnite*!

The random placement of items in *Fortnite* means that every player always has an equal chance to find the best gear. Someone who is playing their first

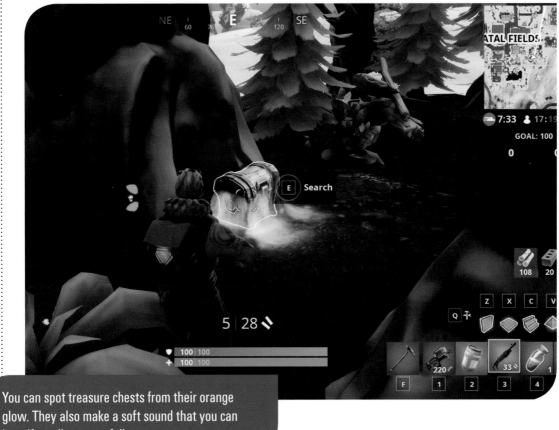

You can spot treasure chests from their orange glow. They also make a soft sound that you can hear if you listen carefully.

Ways to Play

Are you new to *Fortnite*? Maybe you've been hearing about it from your friends and you'd like to try it for yourself. Or maybe you'd like to practice to get as good as your favorite **streamer**. Luckily, it is very easy to dive into the world of *Fortnite*. The game is free to play. It is also available on a wide range of devices. Many people play on desktop or laptop PCs. Others use their tablets or smartphones. You can also play *Fortnite* using a PlayStation 4, Xbox One, or Nintendo Switch video game console.

Even though *Fortnite* is free, be sure to ask a parent or other trusted adult before you start playing. There might be rules they'd like you to follow while playing, or they simply might want to learn more about the game before you start.

match could stumble upon a powerful gun or a chest full of healing items, while experienced players could have trouble finding the items they want. This is good news for beginners. Competition can be tough enough as it is. You never know when you'll find yourself facing off against a pro player. You might have a better chance at winning if you've been lucky enough to come across a powerful weapon.

But how will you know when you've found the best stuff? Which items should you pick up? Which should you ignore? What do all these items even do? Read on to find out everything you need to know to become a master scavenger in *Fortnite*!

Chapter 2

Gathering Your Gear

S o you've safely parachuted out of the Battle Bus and landed on the *Fortnite* island. Now what do you do? The answer is to start scavenging!

As you learned in the previous chapter, you can't predict which items you will find on which parts of

Locations like Tilted Towers are packed full of great items to find, but you will have to compete with a lot of other players who are also searching for the best gear.

Fortnite's in-game map shows all of the island's major named locations.

Fortnite's island. However, you *can* predict which areas of the island are likely to have the best selection of items to choose from. Take a look at the in-game map. You'll notice that some places are marked with names like Tomato Temple, Retail Row, and Tilted Towers. These are usually town-like areas. They contain numerous buildings and underground rooms.

Named areas tend to have a wider variety of items available than wilderness areas. You can search through bedrooms, offices, garages, and basements.

You'll find items on the roofs of skyscrapers and tucked into alleyways. If you visit one of these named areas, you're almost guaranteed to find something good. But don't go rushing right to the nearest one. The downside to visiting a place like Pleasant Park or Paradise Palms is that many other players will have the same plan. As a result, these places often become dangerous battlegrounds. Keep an eye out for other players and be ready to defend yourself if you visit.

Sometimes you will find things just lying on the ground. These will generally be common, easy-to-find items.

A Rainbow of Weapons

You might notice that *Fortnite* weapons glow in different colors. These colors are for more than just looks. They tell you how rare the weapon is. Rarer weapons are generally more powerful than more common ones. They do more damage and can be reloaded faster. Here are what the different colors mean, in order from most common to rarest:

COLOR	RARITY
Gray	Common
Green	Uncommon
Blue	Rare
Purple	Epic
Orange/Gold	Legendary

You can still find plenty of good items if you don't want to visit one of *Fortnite*'s named areas. Even in wilderness areas, you will come across sheds, abandoned cars, and other structures with items inside. Items can also just be lying out in the open. You won't have as many things to choose from. But you could get lucky and find a very useful piece of gear all by itself in the middle of a forest.

Some items you find will simply be floating over the ground. Others are found inside a variety of containers. Ammo boxes contain bullets, rockets,

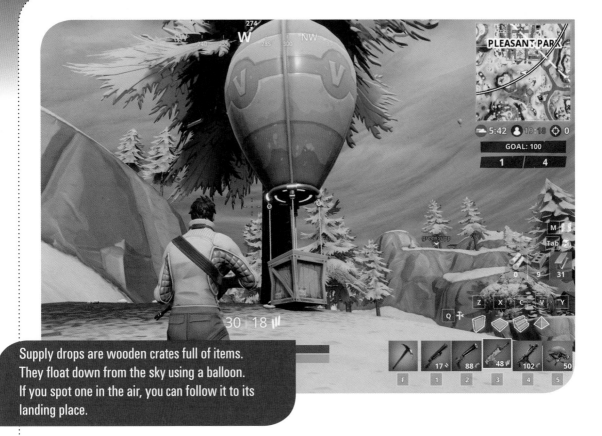

Supply drops are wooden crates full of items. They float down from the sky using a balloon. If you spot one in the air, you can follow it to its landing place.

and other ammo for your weapons. Treasure chests have weapons inside. Supply Llamas are packed with ammo, building materials, and a variety of other items, but they don't have weapons. Supply crates can be filled with almost anything.

Other players are another important source of items. If you are successful in defeating an enemy player, they will drop everything they were carrying. You will be able to pick up any of these items. This is especially helpful near the end of a match, when players are more likely to be carrying very good items.

Early in each match, the things you will need most are good weapons and plenty of ammo. If another player attacks, you'll need to be ready to fight back. You won't stand much of a chance armed with only a pickaxe. Start each match by seeking out a couple of good guns. It is a good idea to pick up the first couple of guns you find, even if they aren't very good. That way you will at least have some way to defend yourself if you get surprised by another player. You can always replace these starter guns as you find better ones later in the match.

Even though weapons are important, don't ignore the other **loot** you find. Healing items such as bandages and medkits are crucial to success. So are shield potions. Be sure to seek all of them out once you have found a useful weapon or two.

Once you've scavenged a few good items, meeting other players won't be quite so risky. You will be able to explore more freely and search for even better items. Always be on the lookout for better gear as you move around the map.

Chapter 3

Searching for Supplies

Scavenging in *Fortnite* is about more than just finding weapons and healing items to help you in combat. It is also about gathering supplies that you can use to build things.

This player is about to run out of building materials. This could make it very hard to win if the match is almost over.

Trees, vehicles, and almost anything else you see in *Fortnite* can all be used to make building materials.

Unlike weapons or healing items, you don't really need a huge amount of building materials right off the bat when you start a new *Fortnite* match. Instead, you will want to gradually gather them as you play. You will usually do most of your building near the end of a match, so you'll want to have a good amount of materials saved up by that point.

There are three types of building materials in *Fortnite*. They are wood, stone, and metal. Wood is the weakest of the three. This means it will be easier for enemy players to destroy the things you build. However, it is also the fastest to build with. This makes it useful when you need to put up a tower or wall as quickly as possible. Metal is the strongest material, but it takes a long time to build with. Stone is right in the middle in terms of both strength and build time.

There are several ways to scavenge for building materials. The first is to simply find them the same way you scavenge for weapons and healing items. Just

You will only find small amounts of building materials on the ground. You will need to use your pickaxe to get larger amounts.

Food on the Forest Floor

As you explore wilderness areas in *Fortnite*, you might spot some small glowing objects on the ground from time to time. Look closer and you'll notice that they are apples and mushrooms. While you wouldn't eat food you found on the ground in real life, you should definitely do it in *Fortnite*. Each apple you eat will restore your health by five points. Each mushroom will restore your shields by five points. Most of the time, several apples or mushrooms are near each other. This means you can get a free, easy boost of 15 or 20 health or shield points. This might not sound like a lot, but it can make a big difference in the long run. Best of all, these items don't take up any space in your **inventory**. Instead, your character will eat them as soon as you pick them up.

like those items, bundles of wood, stone, and metal can be found on the ground or in containers. You can also defeat other players and take the materials they have gathered. But the best and most common way to gather building materials is to use your pickaxe. You can use this helpful tool to break apart almost any object in *Fortnite*'s world. Try knocking down the walls of a house. Bust up an old car parked on the side of a road. Chop down trees. Destroy the towers and walls built by other players.

Every time you break something with your pickaxe, it will produce bundles of building materials. The materials you get will depend on what you destroyed. For example, trees will give you wood, while cars will give you metal.

When you start using your pickaxe on something, you will see a small blue circle appear on-screen. The circle will move around to different locations while you continue to swing your pickaxe. Aim your swings toward this circle. Each time you hit it, your swing will do double damage to the object you are destroying. This will let you destroy objects more quickly. It will also give you more resources. Hitting the circle every time can be tricky, so practice up!

Don't worry about seeking out specific things to break for materials. Instead, simply destroy things as you come across them. Knock over a couple of trees as you sprint through a forest. Destroy a fence instead of jumping over it. Soon enough you will find yourself with a good stock of materials. Be careful, though. Don't start destroying things for building materials when there are other players around. You don't want to be caught swinging your pickaxe at a dumpster when a rival player comes around the corner holding a powerful weapon.

Vending machines sometimes contain very useful loot, so check them out when you find them.

As you explore the *Fortnite* island, you might start to notice colorful vending machines scattered around in different areas. These machines will allow you to trade your extra building materials for a variety of weapons. Each one offers three items—one that is traded for wood, one for stone, and one for metal. Swing your pickaxe at a vending machine to switch between the three items it offers.

The color of the vending machine lets you know the rarity of the items you are trading for. For example, a gray vending machine gives you Common items, while a gold one gives you Legendary items. The amount of materials you need to give the machine is higher for better items. For example, a Legendary rocket launcher might cost 375 materials, while a Common sniper rifle might cost 75. If you have plenty of extra materials to spare, this can be a great way to find useful weapons.

Traps do not take up space in your inventory. They go into a special slot with your buildings materials.

In addition to the three main building materials, you can also scavenge for other items to help you construct defenses. A Port-a-Fort is a useful item that looks somewhat like a grenade. But when you throw it, it doesn't explode. Instead, it instantly builds a three-story metal tower. This is really useful when you need to build quickly. You'll find these helpful items in treasure chests and llamas, much like healing items and weapons.

You can also scavenge for traps. Carry these around and attach them to the walls and floors of your towers and forts to surprise players who try to sneak up on you.

Chapter 4

You Can't Carry Everything!

Successful scavenging in *Fortnite* is about more than just picking up every cool new item you come across. You can only carry five items at a time. Your pickaxe, building materials, traps, and ammo do not count toward this total. However, you will have to make some tough choices when

You can see here that only certain kinds of items will take up valuable equipment slots in your inventory.

Shotguns are usually the best close-range weapons.

deciding which items to pick up and which ones to leave behind.

For example, it is probably not a good idea to fill up all five of your inventory spaces with weapons. Without any health or shield items, you will be in trouble if you take a lot of damage during a fight. Also, it is unlikely that you would need all five weapons at once.

It is helpful to carry weapons that will work in different situations, though. For example, a sniper rifle can help you win long-distance fights, while a shotgun works well up close. Carrying both will ensure that you are ready for anything. It would also leave you with three open inventory slots. You could still have room to carry a grenade, some bandages, and a shield potion.

So what do you do when you have a full inventory and you come across a new item you want to grab? You have two options. First, you can simply pick up

If you're having trouble deciding between weapons, open your inventory and take a closer look at them.

If you are playing as part of a duo or squad, keep your teammates in mind as you scavenge and manage your inventory. Perhaps your friend could use that weapon you were about to toss away. Or maybe your partners are in need of health and you have plenty of medkits. Open your inventory screen and toss the items on the ground. Let your teammates know what you're doing so they can pick up the items. In return, you can ask them for items when you're in need. Sharing gear and supplies is one of the best parts of playing on a team in *Fortnite*.

the new item. If you do this, you will drop whichever inventory item you were carrying and replace it with the new one. To avoid dropping your favorite weapon, switch to the item you need least before grabbing the new item.

You can also open a screen that shows everything you are carrying, from weapons and ammo to building materials. This screen will let you compare the details of each item you are carrying. For example, if you have two guns, you might want to see which one does the most damage. From this screen, you can also drop items to clear space in your inventory.

Try to keep item colors in mind when deciding whether to pick up new weapons. For example,

Improving your scavenging skills is crucial to winning a Victory Royale.

imagine you are carrying a Rare blue weapon. You see an Epic purple weapon of the same type. Should you replace your Rare weapon with the Epic version? Definitely! But now imagine that you are carrying a blue weapon and you see a green one of the same type. You probably don't want to replace your weapon in this case.

If you are carrying shield or health items, use them as soon as you need them. This will make sure your shields and health are always as high as they can be.

It will also help save space in your inventory to pick up more healing items.

Never stop scavenging when you play *Fortnite*. From the moment you land on the island to the final moments of the match, there are always useful new items to find. Search everywhere! The next piece of gear you find could be just what you need to help you win the match.

Glossary

emotes (EE-mohts) animations your character can perform in *Fortnite*

inventory (IN-vuhn-toh-ree) a list of the items your character is carrying

loot (LOOT) the various weapons and other items you can find in *Fortnite*

scavenge (SKAV-uhnj) to search for useful items

skins (SKINZ) different appearances your character can take on in *Fortnite*

streamer (STREE-mur) someone who broadcasts themselves playing video games and talking online

Find Out More

BOOKS

Cunningham, Kevin. *Video Game Designer*. Ann Arbor, MI: Cherry Lake Publishing, 2016.

Powell, Marie. *Asking Questions About Video Games*. Ann Arbor, MI: Cherry Lake Publishing, 2016.

WEBSITES

Epic Games—Fortnite
www.epicgames.com/fortnite/en-US/home
Check out the official *Fortnite* website.

Fortnite Wiki
https://fortnite.gamepedia.com/Fortnite_Wiki
This fan-made website offers up-to-date information on the latest additions to *Fortnite*.

Index

About the Author

Josh Gregory is the author of more than 125 books for kids. He has written about everything from animals to technology to history. A graduate of the University of Missouri–Columbia, he currently lives in Chicago, Illinois.